Practical
Potatoes

p^3

This is a P³ Book
This edition published in 2003

P³
Queen Street House
4 Queen Street
Bath BA1 1HE, UK

ISBN: 1-40540-552-X

Printed in China

NOTE

This book uses metric and imperial measurements. Follow the same units
of measurement throughout; do not mix metric and imperial.
All spoon measurements are level: teaspoons are assumed to be 5 ml, and
tablespoons are assumed to be 15 ml. Unless otherwise stated,
milk is assumed to be full fat, eggs and individual vegetables such as potatoes
are medium, and pepper is freshly ground black pepper.

The nutritional information provided for each recipe is per serving or per person.
Optional ingredients, variations or serving suggestions have
not been included in the calculations. The times given for each recipe are an approximate
guide only because the preparation times may differ according to the techniques used by
different people and the cooking times may vary as a result of the type of oven used.

Recipes using raw or very lightly cooked eggs should be
avoided by children, the elderly, pregnant women, convalescents,
and anyone suffering from an illness.

Contents

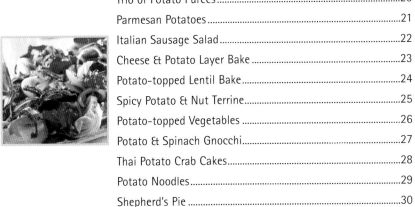

Introduction

Without doubt the potato is the most popular vegetable in the world. On average we eat 109 kg/242 lb per head per annum, which is not surprising since it is one of the most versatile and hardy crops. The potato, first discovered by the Spanish conquistadors in the Andes of Peru, can grow at a higher altitude and in colder climates than any other crop except barley. Moreover, it is said to produce more food per acre than any other northern food crop.

Treasure of the New World

Along with the silver and gold that returned from the New World, potatoes, tomatoes and peppers – which belong to the same botanical family – were to make a huge impact on sixteenth-century Europe. Due to the wide variety of potatoes available, and the fact that they could be cooked in so many different ways, this vegetable became one of the most important food sources on the continent, with Russia, Poland and Germany being the highest consumers.

The vegetable also became famous for its healing and nutritional properties. The Italians believed it could heal a wound if the cooked flesh was rubbed into the infected area. Although this has not withstood the test of time, the nutritional value of this tuber is indisputable. An average-size potato weighing 100 g/3½ oz contains

86 calories, and is rich in carbohydrate, vitamins B and C and fibre, with a tiny amount of protein and some mineral salts (calcium, potassium, iron and iodine).

The variety

Potatoes are starchy tubers and all of them grow underground, several to one plant. The differences in shape, size and texture are enormous. The large Desirée can weigh 450 g/1 lb, while seasonal new potatoes can weigh less than 15 g/½ oz each. The skin-colour range is also vast, from cream and yellow, to brown, pink, red, purple and black, while the skin texture can be smooth or netted. Each potato favours a different method of cooking, although there are also a few all-rounders. This, and the variety in consistencies, lends this vegetable to many uses.

Although there are thousands of different potatoes throughout the world, there are three main types of potato crop – first earlies, second earlies and main-crop. As the name suggests, the earlies are available first, usually from late May, and are often referred to as 'new' potatoes. Main-crop potatoes can be harvested from September until the following June.

This book shows just how many different ways the potato can be prepared. From a natural thickener in soups and pastas, to the principal ingredient in hearty main course dishes, each variety can be put to a multitude of different uses.

KEY	
	Simplicity level 1–3 (1 easiest, 3 slightly harder)
	Preparation time
	Cooking time

Choosing potatoes

When choosing potatoes, always look for the freshest samples. Newly dug potatoes are preferable and to enjoy them at their best they should be eaten soon after purchase. When buying new potatoes, look for skin that rubs away easily. The skin should look tight and smooth, as if the vegetable is bursting with freshness. Main-crop potatoes should, in particular, be free of damage. Always avoid potatoes that are turning green or sprouting, because they have been exposed to too much light and their flavour will be bitter; they will also have higher levels of the natural toxicants called glycoalkaloids. All potatoes should be stored in a cool, dark, airy place.

Selected potato varieties

There are an estimated 3,000 varieties of potato, but of these only about 100 are regularly grown, and only about 20 can be easily found in greengrocers and on supermarket shelves.

- Craig Royal Red: a main-crop potato, ready in July, is non-floury and has a pink or red skin. A waxy potato, it is best for frying and boiling or for using in salads.

- Cyprus New Potato: found in late winter and spring, it is best simply scrubbed and boiled. Not a good mashing potato.
- Desirée: a high-quality, pink-skinned floury potato, good for baking, frying, boiling and mashing.
- Home Guard: generally the first of the new potatoes. It blackens easily and collapses on cooking, so it is best boiled lightly in its skin.
- Jersey Royal: a delicious new potato. It appears from May to October, but is at its peak in August. It has a flaky skin and firm, yellow flesh.
- King Edward: a large potato, which is creamy-white, or sometimes yellow in colour. Ideal for all cooking methods, it is a very popular multipurpose variety.
- Maris Piper: a medium-firm potato with creamy-white flesh. It is good for boiling and frying.
- New Potatoes: these generally have white flesh and grow quickly. They are dug up in early summer and are best scraped and boiled to use in salads or eaten hot with melted butter.
- Pentland Crown: this is a thin-skinned, creamy-white potato, which is at its best in late winter. This potato has a floury texture, making it ideal for mashing and baking.
- Pentland Hawk: a firm, white-fleshed potato, which is suitable for all methods of cooking.
- Pink Fir Apple: this long, knobbly potato has pink flesh and a firm, waxy texture. Good in salads.
- White Sweet Potato: smaller than the yam, although interchangeable, it is yellow-fleshed with a drier texture. Best fried, boiled or cooked in a casserole, it is ideal with spices.
- Yam: a red sweet potato, with orange flesh. It is best mashed in cakes and soufflés or roasted.

Beetroot & Potato Soup

This deep red soup makes a stunning starter – and it's easy to cook in a microwave oven. A swirl of soured cream gives a very pretty effect.

NUTRITIONAL INFORMATION

Calories 120	Sugars 11g
Protein 4g	Fat 2g
Carbohydrate ...22g	Saturates 1g

20 mins   30 mins

SERVES 6

INGREDIENTS

1 onion, chopped

350 g/12 oz potatoes, diced

1 small cooking apple, peeled, cored and grated

3 tbsp water

1 tsp cumin seeds

500 g/1 lb 2 oz cooked beetroot, peeled and diced

1 bay leaf

pinch of dried thyme

1 tsp lemon juice

600 ml/1 pint hot vegetable stock

4 tbsp soured cream

salt and pepper

sprigs of fresh dill, to garnish

1 Place the onion, potatoes, apple and water in a large, microwave-proof bowl. Cover and cook in a microwave oven on HIGH power for 10 minutes. Stir in the cumin seeds and cook on HIGH power for 1 minute.

2 Add the beetroot, bay leaf, thyme, lemon juice and stock. Cover and cook on HIGH power for 12 minutes, stirring halfway through. Set aside, uncovered, for 5 minutes.

3 Remove and discard the bay leaf. Strain the vegetables and reserve the liquid in a jug.

4 Put the vegetables with a little of the reserved liquid in a food processor or blender and process to a smooth and creamy purée. Alternatively, either mash the vegetables with a potato masher or press through a sieve.

5 Pour the vegetable purée into a clean bowl with the reserved liquid and mix well. Season with salt and pepper to taste. Cover and cook on HIGH power for 4–5 minutes until piping hot.

6 Serve the soup in warmed bowls. Swirl 1 tablespoon of soured cream into each bowl and garnish with a few sprigs of fresh dill.

Indian Potato & Pea Soup

A slightly hot and spicy Indian flavour is given to this soup with the use of garam masala, chilli, cumin and coriander.

NUTRITIONAL INFORMATION

Calories	153	Sugars 6g
Protein	. . . . .6g	Fat 6g
Carbohydrate	. . .18g	Saturates 1g

 5 mins   35 mins

SERVES 4

I N G R E D I E N T S

2 tbsp vegetable oil

225 g/8 oz floury potatoes, diced

1 large onion, chopped

2 garlic cloves, crushed

1 tsp garam masala

1 tsp ground coriander

1 tsp ground cumin

900 ml/1½ pints vegetable stock

1 red chilli, chopped

100 g/3½ oz frozen peas

4 tbsp low-fat natural yogurt

salt and pepper

fresh coriander, chopped, to garnish

warm bread, to serve

1 Heat the vegetable oil in a large saucepan and add the diced potatoes, chopped onion and crushed garlic. Sauté gently for 5 minutes, stirring constantly.

2 Add the ground spices and cook for 1 minute, stirring all the time.

3 Stir in the vegetable stock and chopped red chilli and bring the mixture to the boil. Lower the heat, then cover the pan and simmer for 20 minutes until the potatoes begin to break down.

4 Add the peas and cook for another 5 minutes. Stir in the yogurt and season to taste.

5 Pour into warmed soup bowls. Garnish with chopped fresh coriander and serve hot with warm bread.

VARIATION

For slightly less heat, deseed the chilli before adding it to the soup. Always wash your hands after handling chillies because they contain volatile oils that can irritate the skin and make your eyes burn if you touch your face.

Leek, Potato & Carrot Soup

This is a chunky soup, ideal for a snack or a quick lunch. The leftovers can be puréed to make one portion of creamed soup for the next day.

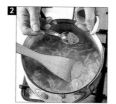

NUTRITIONAL INFORMATION

Calories 156	Sugars 7g
Protein 4g	Fat 6g
Carbohydrate ...22g	Saturates 0.7g

 10 mins   25 mins

SERVES 2

INGREDIENTS

1 leek, about 175 g/6 oz

1 tbsp sunflower oil

1 garlic clove, crushed

700 ml/1¼ pints vegetable stock

1 bay leaf

¼ tsp ground cumin

175 g/6 oz potatoes, diced

125 g/4½ oz carrot, coarsely grated

salt and pepper

fresh parsley, chopped, to garnish

PUREED SOUP

5–6 tbsp milk

1–2 tbsp double cream, crème fraîche or soured cream

1 Trim off and discard some of the coarse green part of the leek, then slice thinly and rinse thoroughly in cold water. Drain well.

2 Heat the sunflower oil in a heavy-based saucepan. Add the leek and garlic and cook over a low heat for about 2–3 minutes until soft but barely coloured. Add the vegetable stock, bay leaf and cumin and then season to taste with salt and pepper. Bring the mixture to the boil, stirring constantly.

3 Add the diced potato to the saucepan, cover and simmer over a low heat for 10–15 minutes until the potato is just tender but not broken up.

4 Add the grated carrot and simmer for another 2–3 minutes. Adjust the seasoning, discard the bay leaf and serve sprinkled liberally with chopped parsley.

5 To make a puréed soup, first process the leftovers (about half the original soup) in a blender or food processor, or press through a sieve until smooth. Return to a clean saucepan with the milk. Bring to the boil and simmer for 2–3 minutes. Adjust the seasoning and stir in the cream, crème fraîche or soured cream before serving sprinkled with chopped parsley.

Potato & Bean Pâté

This pâté is easy to prepare and may be stored in the refrigerator for up to two days. Serve with small toasts, Melba toast or crudités.

NUTRITIONAL INFORMATION

Calories ....94 Sugars 5g
Protein ....6g Fat 1g
Carbohydrate ...17g Saturates 0.2g

5 mins   10 mins

SERVES 4

INGREDIENTS

100 g/3½ oz floury potatoes, peeled and diced

225 g/8 oz canned mixed beans, such as borlotti beans, flageolet beans and kidney beans, drained

1 garlic clove, crushed

2 tsp lime juice

1 tbsp chopped fresh coriander

2 tbsp low-fat natural yogurt

salt and pepper

fresh coriander, chopped, to garnish

1 Cook the potatoes in a pan of boiling water for 10 minutes until tender. Drain well and mash.

2 Transfer the potato to a food processor or blender and add the beans, garlic, lime juice and fresh coriander. Season the mixture and process for 1 minute to make a smooth purée. Alternatively, put the beans in a bowl with the potato, garlic, lime juice and coriander and mash together.

3 If you have used a food processor or blender instead of the hand method, transfer the mixture to a bowl.

4 Add the yogurt and mix well. Spoon the pâté into a serving dish and garnish with the chopped fresh coriander. Serve at once or leave to chill.

COOK'S TIP
To make Melba toast, toast ready-sliced bread lightly on both sides under a preheated hot grill. Remove the crusts. Holding the bread flat, slide a sharp knife through the slice to split it horizontally. Cut into triangles and toast the untoasted side until the edges curl.

Potato & Radish Salad

The radishes and the herb and mustard dressing give this colourful salad a mild mustard flavour, which complements the potatoes perfectly.

NUTRITIONAL INFORMATION

Calories	140	Sugars 3g
Protein	.........3g	Fat 6g
Carbohydrate	...20g	Saturates 1g

 40 mins, plus chilling   15 mins

SERVES 4

I N G R E D I E N T S

500 g/1 lb 2 oz new potatoes, scrubbed and halved

½ cucumber, thinly sliced

2 tsp salt

1 bunch radishes, thinly sliced

D R E S S I N G

1 tbsp Dijon mustard

2 tbsp olive oil

1 tbsp white wine vinegar

2 tbsp chopped mixed herbs

 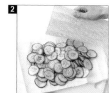 

1 Cook the potatoes in a saucepan of boiling water for 10–15 minutes or until tender. Drain and set aside to cool.

2 Meanwhile, spread out the cucumber on a plate. Sprinkle over the salt. Leave to stand for 30 minutes. Rinse under cold running water. Pat dry with kitchen paper.

3 Arrange the cucumber and radish slices on a serving plate in a decorative pattern and pile the cooked potatoes in the centre of the slices.

4 In a small bowl, mix all the dressing ingredients together, whisking until thoroughly combined. Pour the dressing over the salad, tossing well to coat all of the ingredients. Chill in the refrigerator before serving.

COOK'S TIP

Cucumber adds not only colour but also a real freshness to the salad. It is salted and left to stand to remove the excess water, which would make the salad soggy. Wash the cucumber well to remove all of the salt before adding to the salad.

Potato & Mushroom Hash

This is a quick one-pan dish, which is ideal for a quick snack. It is packed with flavour, and you can add any other vegetables you have to hand.

NUTRITIONAL INFORMATION

Calories 378	Sugars 14g
Protein 18g	Fat 26g
Carbohydrate . . .20g	Saturates 7g

  10 mins   35 mins

SERVES 4

INGREDIENTS

675 g/1½ lb potatoes, cubed

1 tbsp olive oil

2 garlic cloves, crushed

1 green pepper, deseeded and cubed

1 yellow pepper, deseeded and cubed

3 tomatoes, diced

75 g/2¾ oz button mushrooms, halved

1 tbsp Worcestershire sauce

2 tbsp chopped fresh basil

salt and pepper

sprigs of fresh basil, to garnish

warm crusty bread, to serve

1 Cook the potatoes in a saucepan of boiling salted water for 7–8 minutes. Drain well and reserve.

2 Heat the olive oil in a large, heavy-based frying pan. Add the boiled potatoes and cook for 8–10 minutes, stirring, until browned.

3 Add the garlic and peppers to the frying pan and cook for 2–3 minutes.

4 Add the tomatoes and mushrooms and cook, stirring, for 5–6 minutes.

5 Stir in the Worcestershire sauce and chopped basil and season well. Garnish with the sprigs of fresh basil and serve with warm crusty bread.

COOK'S TIP
Most brands of Worcestershire sauce contain anchovies. If you are cooking for vegetarians, make sure you choose a vegetarian variety.

Potato & Spinach Triangles

These small triangles are made with crisp filo pastry and filled with a tasty spinach and potato mixture flavoured with chilli and tomato.

NUTRITIONAL INFORMATION

Calories 514	Sugars 4g
Protein 9g	Fat 37g
Carbohydrate . . .37g	Saturates 8g

 25 mins   35 mins

SERVES 4

INGREDIENTS

2 tbsp butter, melted, plus extra
for greasing

225 g/8 oz waxy potatoes, finely diced

500 g/1 lb 2 oz baby spinach

1 tomato, deseeded and chopped

¼ tsp chilli powder

½ tsp lemon juice

225 g/8 oz filo pastry, thawed if frozen

salt and pepper

crisp salad, to serve

LEMON MAYONNAISE

150 ml/5 fl oz mayonnaise

2 tsp lemon juice

zest of 1 lemon

1 Lightly grease a baking tray with a little melted butter.

2 Cook the potatoes in a saucepan of lightly salted boiling water for about 10 minutes or until cooked through. Drain thoroughly and place in a mixing bowl.

3 Meanwhile, put the spinach in a saucepan with 2 tablespoonfuls of water. Cover and cook over a low heat for 2 minutes until wilted. Drain the spinach thoroughly, squeezing out excess moisture, and add to the potato.

4 Stir in the chopped tomato, chilli powder and lemon juice. Season to taste with salt and pepper.

5 Lightly brush 8 sheets of filo pastry with melted butter. Spread out 4 of the sheets and lay the other 4 on top. Cut them into rectangles measuring about 20 x 10 cm/8 x 4 inches.

6 Spoon some of the potato and spinach mixture onto one end of each rectangle. Fold a corner of the pastry over the filling, fold the pointed end back over the pastry strip then fold over the remaining pastry to form a triangle.

7 Place the triangles on the baking tray and bake in a preheated oven, 190°C/375°F/Gas Mark 5, for 20 minutes or until golden brown.

8 To make the mayonnaise, mix the mayonnaise, lemon juice and lemon zest together in a small bowl. Serve the potato and spinach triangles warm or cold with the lemon mayonnaise and a crisp salad.

Potatoes En Papillotes

New potatoes are perfect for this recipe. The potatoes and vegetables are wrapped in greaseproof paper and sealed, then steamed in the oven.

NUTRITIONAL INFORMATION

Calories ....85 Sugars 4g
Protein ....2g Fat 0.5g
Carbohydrate ...15g Saturates 0.1g

 10 mins   35 mins

SERVES 4

I N G R E D I E N T S

450 g/1 lb small new potatoes

1 carrot, cut into thin sticks

1 fennel bulb, sliced

75 g/2¾ oz French beans

1 yellow pepper, cut into strips

250 ml/9 fl oz dry white wine

4 sprigs of fresh rosemary

salt and pepper

sprigs of fresh rosemary, to garnish

1 Cut out 4 squares of greaseproof paper, each square measuring about 25 cm/ 10 inches in size.

2 Divide the vegetables equally between the 4 paper squares, placing them in the centre of each square.

3 Bring the edges of the paper inwards and scrunch them together to encase the vegetables, but leave the tops open.

4 Place the parcels in a shallow roasting tin and spoon 4 tablespoons of white wine into each parcel. Add a rosemary sprig and seasoning.

5 Fold the top of each parcel over to seal it. Cook them in a preheated oven, 190°C/375°F/Gas Mark 5, for 30–35 minutes or until the vegetables are tender.

6 Transfer the sealed parcels to 4 individual serving plates and garnish with rosemary sprigs.

7 Open the parcels at the table so that the full aroma of the vegetables can be appreciated.

COOK'S TIP

If small new potatoes are unavailable, use larger potatoes that have been halved or cut into quarters to ensure that they cook through in the specified cooking time.

Mixed Mushroom Cakes

These cakes are packed with creamy potato and a variety of mushrooms and will be loved by vegetarians and meat-eaters alike.

NUTRITIONAL INFORMATION

Calories	298	Sugars	.......0.8g
Protein	........5g	Fat	.........22g
Carbohydrate	...22g	Saturates	.......5g

20 mins   25 mins

SERVES 4

I N G R E D I E N T S

500 g/1 lb 2 oz floury potatoes, peeled and diced

2 tbsp butter

175 g/6 oz mixed mushrooms, chopped

2 garlic cloves, crushed

1 small egg, beaten

1 tbsp chopped fresh chives, plus extra to garnish

flour, for dusting

vegetable oil, for cooking

salt and pepper

crisp salad, to serve

1 Cook the potatoes in a saucepan of lightly salted boiling water for 10 minutes or until cooked through.

2 Drain the potatoes well, mash with a potato masher or fork and set aside.

3 Meanwhile, melt the butter in a frying pan. Add the mushrooms and garlic and cook over a medium heat, stirring constantly, for 5 minutes. Drain well.

4 Stir the mushrooms and garlic into the potatoes, together with the beaten egg and chives.

5 Divide the mixture equally into 4 portions and shape them into round cakes. Toss them in the flour until the outsides of the cakes are completely coated, shaking off any excess.

6 Heat the oil in a frying pan. Add the mushroom cakes and cook over a medium heat for 10 minutes until they are golden brown, turning them over halfway through. Season. Serve the cakes immediately with a simple crisp salad.

COOK'S TIP

Prepare the cakes in advance, cover with clingfilm and then set aside to chill in the refrigerator for up to 24 hours, if you wish.

Feta & Spinach Omelette

This quick chunky omelette has pieces of potato cooked into
the egg mixture and is then filled with feta cheese and spinach.

NUTRITIONAL INFORMATION

Calories 564   Sugars 6g
Protein . . . . .30g   Fat 39g
Carbohydrate . . .25g   Saturates 19g

20 mins   25–30 mins

SERVES 4

I N G R E D I E N T S

6 tbsp butter

1.3 kg/3 lb waxy potatoes, diced

3 garlic cloves, crushed

1 tsp paprika

2 tomatoes, skinned, deseeded and diced

12 eggs

pepper

F I L L I N G

225 g/8 oz baby spinach

1 tsp fennel seeds

125 g/4½ oz feta cheese (drained
weight), diced

4 tbsp natural yogurt

1 Heat 2 tablespoons of the butter in a
frying pan and cook the potatoes over
a low heat, stirring, for 7–10 minutes until
golden. Transfer to a bowl.

2 Add the garlic, paprika and tomatoes
to the frying pan and cook for
another 2 minutes.

3 Whisk the eggs together and season
with pepper. Pour the eggs into the
potatoes and mix well.

4 Cook the spinach in boiling water for
1 minute until just wilted. Drain and

refresh under cold running water. Pat dry
with kitchen paper. Stir in the fennel
seeds, feta cheese and yogurt.

5 Heat one-quarter of the remaining
butter in a 15-cm/6-inch omelette
pan. Ladle one-quarter of the egg and
potato mixture into the pan. Cook, turning
once, for 2 minutes until set.

6 Transfer to a serving plate. Spoon one-
quarter of the spinach mixture onto
half of the omelette, then fold the omelette
in half over the filling. Repeat steps 5 and 6
to make 4 omelettes.

VARIATION
Use any other cheese, such as
blue cheese, instead of the feta,
and blanched broccoli in place of
the baby spinach, if you prefer.

Hash Browns

Hash browns are a popular dish of fried potato squares, often served as brunch. This recipe includes extra vegetables.

NUTRITIONAL INFORMATION

Calories ....339 Sugars 9g
Protein ....10g Fat 21g
Carbohydrate ...29g Saturates 7g

 20 mins 🕑 45 mins

SERVES 4

INGREDIENTS

500 g/1 lb 2 oz waxy potatoes, peeled

1 carrot, diced

1 celery stick, diced

60 g/2¼ oz button mushrooms, diced

1 onion, diced

2 garlic cloves, crushed

25 g/1 oz frozen peas, thawed

60 g/2¼ oz Parmesan cheese, freshly grated

4 tbsp vegetable oil

2 tbsp butter

salt and pepper

SAUCE

300 ml/10 fl oz passata

2 tbsp chopped fresh coriander

1 tbsp Worcestershire sauce

½ tsp chilli powder

2 tsp brown sugar

2 tsp mild mustard

5 tbsp vegetable stock

1 Cook the potatoes in a saucepan of lightly salted boiling water for 10 minutes. Drain and set aside to cool. Meanwhile, cook the carrot in lightly salted boiling water for 5 minutes.

2 When the potatoes are cool enough to handle, grate them with a coarse grater.

3 Drain the carrot and add it to the grated potatoes, along with the celery, mushrooms, onion, garlic, peas and cheese. Season to taste with salt and pepper.

4 Put all of the sauce ingredients in a small saucepan and bring to the boil. Reduce the heat to low and simmer for 15 minutes.

5 Divide the potato mixture into 8 portions of equal size and shape into flattened rectangles with your hands.

6 Heat the oil and butter in a frying pan and cook the hash browns in batches over a low heat for about 4–5 minutes on each side until crisp and golden brown.

7 Transfer the hash browns to a serving plate and serve immediately with the tomato sauce.

Souffléd Cheesy Potato Fries

These small potato chunks are mixed in a creamy cheese sauce and cooked in oil until deliciously golden brown.

NUTRITIONAL INFORMATION

Calories 614   Sugars 2g
Protein . . . . .12g   Fat 46g
Carbohydrate . . .40g   Saturates 18g

20 mins   25 mins

SERVES 4

I N G R E D I E N T S

900 g/2 lb potatoes, cut into chunks

150 ml/5 fl oz double cream

75 g/2¾ oz Gruyère cheese, grated

pinch of cayenne pepper

2 egg whites

vegetable oil, for deep-frying

salt and pepper

TO GARNISH

chopped fresh flat-leaved parsley

grated cheese

1 Cook the potatoes in a saucepan of lightly salted boiling water for about 10 minutes. Drain thoroughly and pat dry with absorbent kitchen paper. Set aside until required.

2 Mix the double cream and Gruyère cheese in a large bowl. Stir in the cayenne pepper and season with salt and pepper to taste.

3 Whisk the egg whites until stiff peaks form. Gently fold into the cheese mixture until fully incorporated.

4 Add the cooked potatoes, turning to coat thoroughly in the mixture.

5 In a deep pan, heat the oil to 180°C/350°F or until a cube of bread browns in 30 seconds. Remove the potatoes from the cheese mixture with a slotted spoon and cook them in the oil, in batches if necessary, for 3–4 minutes or until golden.

6 Transfer the potatoes to a warmed serving dish and garnish with parsley and grated cheese. Serve immediately.

VARIATION

Add other flavourings, such as grated nutmeg or curry powder, to the cream and cheese.

Bubble & Squeak

Bubble and squeak is best known as fried mashed potato and leftover greens served together as an accompaniment.

NUTRITIONAL INFORMATION

Calories	301	Sugars	..........5g
Protein	........11g	Fat	..........18g
Carbohydrate	...24g	Saturates	.......2g

15 mins   40 mins

SERVES 4

INGREDIENTS

450 g/1 lb floury potatoes, peeled and diced

225 g/8 oz Savoy cabbage, shredded

5 tbsp vegetable oil

2 leeks, chopped

1 garlic clove, crushed

225 g/8 oz smoked tofu, cubed

salt and pepper

shredded cooked leek, to garnish

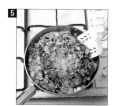

1 Cook the diced potatoes in a saucepan of lightly salted boiling water for 10 minutes until tender. Drain and mash the potatoes.

2 Meanwhile, in a separate saucepan, blanch the cabbage in boiling water for 5 minutes. Drain well and add to the potato.

3 Heat the oil in a heavy-based frying pan. Add the leeks and garlic and cook gently for 2–3 minutes. Stir into the potato and cabbage mixture.

4 Add the smoked tofu and season well with salt and pepper. Cook over a medium heat for 10 minutes.

5 Carefully turn the whole mixture over and continue to cook over a medium heat for another 5–7 minutes until crispy underneath. Serve immediately, garnished with shredded leek.

COOK'S TIP

This vegetarian version is a perfect main meal, because the smoked tofu cubes added to the basic bubble and squeak mixture make it very substantial and nourishing.

Spiced Potatoes & Spinach

This is a classic Indian accompaniment for many different curries or plainer main vegetable dishes. It is very quick to cook.

NUTRITIONAL INFORMATION

Calories	176	Sugars	.........4g
Protein	.........6g	Fat	...........9g
Carbohydrate	...18g	Saturates	.......1g

 10 mins 20 mins

SERVES 4

INGREDIENTS

3 tbsp vegetable oil

1 red onion, sliced

2 garlic cloves, crushed

½ tsp chilli powder

2 tsp ground coriander

1 tsp ground cumin

150 ml/5 fl oz vegetable stock

300 g/10½ oz potatoes, diced

500 g/1 lb 2 oz baby spinach

1 red chilli, deseeded and sliced

salt and pepper

1 Heat the oil in a heavy-based frying pan. Add the onion and garlic and then sauté over a medium heat, stirring occasionally, for 2–3 minutes.

2 Stir in the chilli powder, ground coriander and cumin and cook, stirring constantly, for another 30 seconds.

3 Add the vegetable stock, diced potatoes and spinach and bring to the boil. Lower the heat, cover the frying pan and simmer for about 10 minutes or until the potatoes are cooked right through and tender.

4 Uncover and season to taste with salt and pepper, then add the chilli and cook for another 2–3 minutes. Transfer to a warmed serving dish and serve immediately.

COOK'S TIP
Besides adding extra colour to a dish, red onions have a sweeter, less pungent flavour than other varieties.

Trio of Potato Purées

These small moulds filled with layers of flavoured potato look very impressive. They are ideal with fish or roasted meats.

NUTRITIONAL INFORMATION

Calories	170	Sugars	5g
Protein	7g	Fat	6g
Carbohydrate	24g	Saturates	3g

15 mins   1¼ hrs

SERVES 4

I N G R E D I E N T S

1 tbsp butter, plus extra for greasing

300 g/10½ oz floury potatoes, peeled and chopped

125 g/4½ oz swede, chopped

1 carrot, chopped

450 g/1 lb spinach

1 tbsp skimmed milk

2½ tbsp plain flour

1 egg

½ tsp ground cinnamon

1 tbsp orange juice

¼ tsp grated nutmeg

salt and pepper

1 carrot, cut into thin sticks, to garnish

1 Lightly grease four 150-ml/5-fl oz ramekins with butter.

2 Cook the potatoes in a saucepan of boiling water for 10 minutes. In separate saucepans, cook the swede and carrot in boiling water for 10 minutes. Blanch the spinach in boiling water for 5 minutes. Drain the vegetables. Add the milk and butter to the potatoes and mash until smooth. Stir in the flour and egg.

3 Divide the potato mixture into 3 bowls. Spoon the swede into one bowl and mix well. Spoon the carrot into the second bowl and mix well. Spoon the spinach into the third bowl and mix well.

4 Add the cinnamon to the swede and potato mixture and season to taste. Stir the orange juice into the carrot and potato mixture. Stir the nutmeg into the spinach and potato mixture.

5 Spoon a layer of the swede and potato mixture into each of the ramekins and smooth over the tops. Cover each with a layer of spinach and potato mixture, then top with the carrot and potato mixture. Cover the ramekins with foil and place in a roasting tin. Half-fill the pan with boiling water and cook in a preheated oven, 180°C/350°F/Gas Mark 4, for 40 minutes or until set.

6 Turn out onto serving plates. Garnish with the thin carrot sticks and then serve immediately.

Parmesan Potatoes

This is a very simple way to jazz up roast potatoes. The bacon and Parmesan cheese add a delicious flavour in this recipe.

NUTRITIONAL INFORMATION

Calories 307	Sugars 2g
Protein 11g	Fat 14g
Carbohydrate . . .37g	Saturates 6g

🥔 15 mins   🕐 1 hr 5 mins

SERVES 4

I N G R E D I E N T S

1.3 kg/3 lb potatoes

50 g/1¾ oz Parmesan cheese, grated

pinch of grated nutmeg

1 tbsp chopped fresh parsley

4 smoked bacon slices, cut into strips

vegetable oil, for roasting

salt

1 Cut the potatoes in half lengthways and cook them in a saucepan of boiling salted water for 10 minutes. Drain them thoroughly.

2 Mix the grated Parmesan cheese, nutmeg and parsley together in a shallow bowl.

3 Roll the potato pieces in the cheese mixture to coat them completely. Shake off any excess.

4 Pour a little oil into a roasting tin and heat it in a preheated oven, 200°C/400°F/Gas Mark 6, for 10 minutes. Remove from the oven and place the potatoes in the tin. Return the tin to the oven and cook for 30 minutes, turning once.

5 Remove from the oven and scatter the bacon on top of the potatoes. Return to the oven for 15 minutes or until the potatoes and bacon are cooked. Drain off any excess fat and serve.

VARIATION

If you prefer, use slices of salami or Parma ham instead of the bacon, adding it to the dish 5 minutes before the end of the cooking time.

Italian Sausage Salad

Sliced Italian sausage blends well with the other Mediterranean flavours of sun-dried tomato and basil in this salad.

NUTRITIONAL INFORMATION

Calories 450	Sugars 6g	
Protein 13g	Fat 28g	
Carbohydrate ...38g	Saturates 1g	

 25 mins   25 mins

SERVES 4

INGREDIENTS

450 g/1 lb waxy potatoes

1 radicchio or lollo rosso lettuce

1 green pepper, deseeded and sliced

175 g/6 oz Italian sausage, sliced

1 red onion, halved and sliced

125 g/4½ oz sun-dried tomatoes, sliced

2 tbsp shredded fresh basil

DRESSING

1 tbsp balsamic vinegar

1 tsp tomato purée

2 tbsp olive oil

salt and pepper

COOK'S TIP

Any sliced Italian sausage or salami can be used in this salad. Italy is home of the salami and there are numerous varieties to choose from – those from the south tend to be more highly spiced than those from the north of the country.

1 Cook the potatoes in a saucepan of boiling water for 20 minutes or until cooked through. Drain and leave to cool.

2 Line a large serving platter with the radicchio or lollo rosso lettuce.

3 Slice the cooled potatoes and arrange them in layers on the lettuce-lined serving platter together with the sliced green pepper, sliced Italian sausage, red onion, sun-dried tomatoes and shredded fresh basil.

4 In a small bowl, whisk together the balsamic vinegar, tomato puree and olive oil and season to taste with salt and pepper. Pour the dressing over the potato salad and serve immediately.

Cheese & Potato Layer Bake

This is a quick dish to prepare and it can be left to cook in the oven without needing any more attention.

NUTRITIONAL INFORMATION

Calories . . . . . . .766 Sugars 14g
Protein . . . . .44g Fat 40g
Carbohydrate . . .60g Saturates 23g

25 mins   45 mins

SERVES 4

I N G R E D I E N T S

900 g/2 lb unpeeled waxy potatoes,
   cut into wedges

2 tbsp butter

1 red onion, halved and sliced

2 garlic cloves, crushed

2½ tbsp plain flour

600 ml/1 pint milk

400 g/14 oz canned artichoke hearts in
   brine, drained and halved

150 g/5½ oz frozen mixed vegetables,
   thawed

125 g/4½ oz Gruyère cheese, grated

125 g/4½ oz mature cheese, grated

50 g/1¾ oz Gorgonzola, crumbled

25 g/1 oz Parmesan cheese, freshly grated

225 g/8 oz tofu, sliced

2 tbsp chopped fresh thyme

salt and pepper

sprigs of fresh thyme, to garnish

1 Cook the potato wedges in a saucepan of boiling water for 10 minutes. Drain thoroughly.

2 Meanwhile, melt the butter in a saucepan. Add the sliced onion and garlic and cook over a low heat, stirring frequently, for 2–3 minutes.

3 Stir the flour into the pan and cook, stirring constantly, for 1 minute. Gradually add the milk and bring to the boil, still stirring constantly.

4 Lower the heat and add the artichoke hearts, mixed vegetables, half of each of the 4 cheeses, and the tofu to the pan and mix well. Stir in the chopped thyme and season with salt and pepper to taste.

5 Arrange a layer of parboiled potato wedges in the bottom of a shallow, ovenproof dish. Spoon the vegetable mixture over the top and cover with the remaining potato wedges. Sprinkle the rest of the 4 cheeses over the top.

6 Cook in a preheated oven, 200°C/400°F/Gas Mark 6, for 30 minutes or until the potatoes are cooked and the top is golden brown. Serve garnished with fresh thyme sprigs.

Potato-topped Lentil Bake

This wonderful mixture of red lentils, tofu and vegetables is cooked beneath a crunchy potato topping for a really hearty meal.

NUTRITIONAL INFORMATION

Calories . . . . . . .627 Sugars 7g
Protein . . . . .26g Fat 30g
Carbohydrate . . .66g Saturates 13g

🄖 🄖 🄖

🔺 10 mins   🕐 1½ hours

SERVES 4

I N G R E D I E N T S

675 g/1½ lb floury potatoes, peeled

2 tbsp butter

1 tbsp milk

50 g/1¾ oz pecan nuts, chopped

2 tbsp chopped fresh thyme

sprigs of fresh thyme, to garnish

FILLING

225 g/8 oz red lentils

4 tbsp butter

1 leek, sliced

2 garlic cloves, crushed

1 celery stick, chopped

125 g/4½ oz broccoli florets

175 g/6 oz smoked tofu, cubed

2 tsp tomato purée

salt and pepper

1 Dice the potatoes and cook in a saucepan of boiling water for about 10–15 minutes or until cooked through. Drain well. Add the butter and milk and mash thoroughly. Stir in the pecan nuts and chopped thyme and then set aside.

2 Cook the lentils in boiling water for 20–30 minutes or until tender. Drain and set aside.

3 Melt the butter in a frying pan. Add the leek, garlic, celery and broccoli. Cook over a medium heat, stirring frequently, for 5 minutes until softened. Add the tofu cubes. Stir in the lentils, together with the tomato purée. Season with salt and pepper to taste, then turn the mixture into the bottom of a shallow, ovenproof dish.

4 Spoon the mashed potato on top of the lentil mixture, spreading to cover it completely.

5 Cook in a preheated oven, 200°C/400°F/Gas Mark 6, for 30–35 minutes or until the topping is golden. Garnish with sprigs of fresh thyme and serve hot.

VARIATION

You can use almost any combination of your favourite vegetables in this dish.

Spicy Potato & Nut Terrine

This delicious baked terrine has a base of mashed potato flavoured with nuts, cheese, herbs and spices.

NUTRITIONAL INFORMATION

Calories . . . . . . .1100 Sugars 13g
Protein . . . . .34g Fat 93g
Carbohydrate . . .31g Saturates 22g

 15 mins 1½ hrs

SERVES 4

I N G R E D I E N T S

2 tbsp butter, plus extra for greasing

225 g/8 oz floury potatoes, peeled and diced

225 g/8 oz shelled pecan nuts

225 g/8 oz unsalted cashew nuts

1 onion, finely chopped

2 garlic cloves, crushed

115 g/4 oz open-cap mushrooms, diced

2 tbsp chopped fresh mixed herbs

1 tsp paprika

1 tsp ground cumin

1 tsp ground coriander

4 eggs, beaten

125 g/4½ oz full-fat soft cheese

60 g/2¼ oz Parmesan cheese, freshly grated

salt and pepper

S A U C E

3 large tomatoes, skinned, deseeded and chopped

2 tbsp tomato purée

5 tbsp red wine

1 tbsp red wine vinegar

pinch of caster sugar

1 Lightly grease a 900-g/2-lb loaf tin with a little butter and line it with baking paper.

2 Cook the potatoes in a large saucepan of lightly salted boiling water for 10 minutes or until cooked through. Drain and mash thoroughly.

3 Finely chop the pecan nuts and cashew nuts or process in a food processor. Mix the nuts in a bowl with the onion, garlic and mushrooms. Melt the butter in a frying pan and cook the nut mixture for 5–7 minutes. Add the herbs and spices. Stir in the eggs, cheeses and potatoes and season to taste with salt and pepper.

4 Spoon the mixture into the prepared loaf tin, pressing it down quite firmly. Cook in a preheated oven, 190°C/375°F/Gas Mark 5, for 1 hour or until set.

5 To make the sauce, mix the tomatoes, tomato purée, wine, wine vinegar and sugar in a pan and bring to the boil, stirring constantly. Cook for 10 minutes or until the tomatoes have reduced. Press the sauce through a sieve or process in a food processor for 30 seconds. Turn the terrine out of the pan onto a serving plate and cut into slices. Serve with the tomato sauce.

Potato-topped Vegetables

This is a very colourful and nutritious dish, packed full of crunchy vegetables in a tasty white wine sauce.

NUTRITIONAL INFORMATION

Calories 413   Sugars 11g
Protein . . . . .19g   Fat 18g
Carbohydrate . . .41g   Saturates 11g

🍲 20 mins   🕐 1¼ hrs

SERVES 4

INGREDIENTS

1 carrot, diced

175 g/6 oz cauliflower florets

175 g/6 oz broccoli florets

1 fennel bulb, sliced

85 g/3 oz French beans, halved

2 tbsp butter

2½ tbsp plain flour

150 ml/5 fl oz vegetable stock

150 ml/5 fl oz dry white wine

150 ml/5 fl oz milk

175 g/6 oz chestnut mushrooms, cut into quarters

2 tbsp chopped fresh sage

TOPPING

900 g/2 lb floury potatoes, peeled and diced

2 tbsp butter

4 tbsp natural yogurt

4 tbsp freshly grated Parmesan cheese

1 tsp fennel seeds

salt and pepper

1 Cook the carrot, cauliflower, broccoli, fennel and French beans in a large saucepan of boiling water for 10 minutes until just tender. Drain the vegetables thoroughly and set aside.

2 Melt the butter in a saucepan. Stir in the flour and cook for 1 minute. Remove from the heat and stir in the stock, wine and milk. Return to the heat and bring to the boil, stirring, until thickened. Stir in the vegetables, mushrooms and sage.

3 Meanwhile, make the topping. Cook the potatoes in boiling water for 10–15 minutes. Drain thoroughly and mash with the butter, yogurt and half the grated cheese. Stir in the fennel seeds. Season to taste.

4 Spoon the vegetable mixture into a 1-litre/1¾-pint pie dish. Spoon the mashed potato over the top and sprinkle over the remaining cheese. Cook in a preheated oven, 190°C/375°F/Gas Mark 5, for 30–35 minutes until golden. Serve hot.

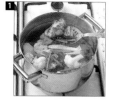
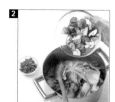

Potato & Spinach Gnocchi

These small potato dumplings are flavoured with spinach, cooked in boiling water and served with a simple tomato sauce.

NUTRITIONAL INFORMATION

Calories 315   Sugars 7g
Protein . . . . .8g   Fat 8g
Carbohydrate . . .56g   Saturates 1g

🧊 20 mins   🕐 30 mins

SERVES 4

I N G R E D I E N T S

300 g/10½ oz floury potatoes, peeled

175 g/6 oz spinach, plus extra to garnish

1 egg yolk

1 tsp olive oil

125 g/4½ oz plain flour

salt and pepper

S A U C E

1 tbsp olive oil

2 shallots, chopped

1 garlic clove, crushed

300 ml/10 fl oz passata

2 tsp soft light brown sugar

1 Dice the potatoes and put them in a saucepan of boiling water. Cook them for 10 minutes or until cooked through. Drain and mash the potatoes.

2 Meanwhile, in a separate pan, blanch the spinach in a little boiling water for 1–2 minutes. Drain and shred the leaves.

3 Transfer the potato to a floured chopping board. Make a well in the centre. Add the egg yolk, olive oil, spinach and a little of the flour. Quickly mix the ingredients into the potato, adding more flour as you go, until you have a firm dough. Divide into very small dumplings.

4 Put the gnocchi in a saucepan of boiling salted water and cook for 5 minutes or until they rise to the surface (you may need to do this in batches).

5 Meanwhile, make the sauce. Put the olive oil, shallots, garlic, passata and sugar into a saucepan and cook over a low heat for 10–15 minutes or until the sauce has thickened.

6 Use a slotted spoon to drain the gnocchi, then transfer to warm serving dishes. Spoon the sauce over the gnocchi and garnish with the fresh spinach leaves.

VARIATION
Add chopped fresh herbs and grated cheese to the gnocchi dough instead of the spinach, if you prefer.

Thai Potato Crab Cakes

These crab cakes are based on a traditional Thai recipe. They make a delicious snack when served with this sweet-and-sour cucumber sauce.

NUTRITIONAL INFORMATION

Calories 254	Sugars 9g
Protein 12g	Fat 6g
Carbohydrate . . .40g	Saturates 1g

  10 mins   30 mins

SERVES 4

I N G R E D I E N T S

450 g/1 lb floury potatoes, peeled

175 g/6 oz white crab meat, drained if canned

4 spring onions, chopped

1 tsp light soy sauce

½ tsp sesame oil

1 tsp chopped lemon grass

1 tsp lime juice

3 tbsp plain flour

2 tbsp vegetable oil

salt and pepper

S A U C E

4 tbsp finely chopped cucumber

2 tbsp honey

1 tbsp garlic wine vinegar

½ tsp light soy sauce

1 red chilli, deseeded and chopped

T O   G A R N I S H

1 red chilli, deseeded and sliced

cucumber slices

1 Dice the potatoes and cook in a pan of boiling water for 10 minutes until cooked through. Drain well and mash.

2 Mix the crab meat into the potato with the spring onions, soy sauce, sesame oil, lemon grass, lime juice and flour. Season with salt and pepper.

3 Divide the crab and potato mixture into 8 equal portions and shape them into small rounds, using floured hands.

4 Heat the oil in a wok or frying pan and cook the cakes, in batches of 4 at a time, for 5–7 minutes, turning once.

Remove from the pan with a palette knife and keep warm.

5 Meanwhile, make the sauce. In a small serving bowl, mix the cucumber, honey, vinegar, soy sauce and chilli.

6 Garnish the cakes with the sliced red chilli and cucumber and serve with the sauce.

Potato Noodles

In this recipe, potatoes are used to make a dough, which is cut into thin noodles and boiled. These are served with a creamy bacon sauce.

NUTRITIONAL INFORMATION

Calories 810   Sugars 5g
Protein . . . . .21g   Fat 47g
Carbohydrate . . .81g   Saturates 26g

20 mins   20 mins

SERVES 4

I N G R E D I E N T S

450 g/1 lb floury potatoes, peeled

225 g/8 oz plain flour

1 egg, beaten

1 tbsp milk

salt and pepper

sprigs of fresh parsley, to garnish

S A U C E

1 tbsp vegetable oil

1 onion, chopped

1 garlic clove, crushed

125 g/4½ oz open-cup mushrooms, sliced

3 slices smoked bacon, chopped

50 g/1¾ oz Parmesan cheese, freshly grated

300 ml/10 fl oz double cream

2 tbsp chopped fresh parsley

1 Dice the potatoes and cook in a saucepan of boiling water for about 10 minutes until cooked through. Drain well. Mash the potatoes until smooth, then beat in the flour, egg and milk. Season with salt and pepper to taste and bring together to form a stiff paste.

2 On a lightly floured work surface, roll out the paste to form a long, thin sausage shape. Cut the sausage into 2.5-cm/1-inch lengths. Bring a large saucepan of salted water to the boil, drop in the dough pieces and cook for 3–4 minutes. They will rise to the top when cooked.

3 To make the sauce, heat the oil in a pan and sauté the onion and garlic for 2 minutes. Add the mushrooms and bacon and cook for 5 minutes. Stir in the cheese, cream and parsley, and season.

4 Drain the noodles and transfer to a warm pasta bowl. Spoon the sauce over the top and toss to mix. Garnish with parsley sprigs and serve.

COOK'S TIP

Make the dough in advance, then wrap and store the noodles in the refrigerator for up to 24 hours.

Shepherd's Pie

This pie can be made with minced lamb or beef. It is cooked with onions, carrots, herbs and tomatoes and has a creamy potato topping.

NUTRITIONAL INFORMATION

Calories 378	Sugars 8g
Protein 33g	Fat 12g
Carbohydrate ...37g	Saturates 4g

🄖 🄖 🄖

🍲 10 mins   🕐 1¹/₂ hours

SERVES 4–5

INGREDIENTS

700 g/1 lb 9 oz minced lean lamb or beef

2 onions, chopped

225 g/8 oz carrots, diced

1–2 garlic cloves, crushed

1 tbsp plain flour

200 ml/7 fl oz beef stock

200 g/7 oz canned chopped tomatoes

1 tsp Worcestershire sauce

1 tsp chopped fresh sage or oregano, or
  ½ tsp dried sage or oregano

750 g–1 kg/1 lb 10 oz–2 lb 4 oz potatoes

2 tbsp margarine

3–4 tbsp skimmed milk

125 g/4½ oz button mushrooms, sliced
  (optional)

salt and pepper

1 Place the meat in a heavy-based saucepan with no extra fat and cook gently, stirring frequently, until the meat begins to brown.

2 Add the onions, carrots and garlic and continue to cook gently for about 10 minutes. Stir in the flour and cook for a minute or so, then gradually stir in the stock and tomatoes and bring to the boil.

3 Add the Worcestershire sauce, seasoning and herbs, cover the pan and simmer gently for about 25 minutes, giving an occasional stir.

4 Peel and dice the potatoes and cook in boiling salted water until tender, then drain thoroughly and mash. Beat in the margarine, seasoning and sufficient milk to give a smooth consistency. Place in a piping bag fitted with a large, star-shaped nozzle.

5 Stir the mushrooms, if using, into the meat and adjust the seasoning. Transfer to a shallow, ovenproof dish.

6 Pipe the potatoes evenly over the meat. Cook in a preheated oven at 200°C/400°F/Gas Mark 6 for about 30 minutes until hot and the potatoes are golden brown.

VARIATION

If you prefer, you can mix boiled potatoes with parsnips or swede for the topping in this recipe.

Lamb & Potato Masala

To create delicious Indian dishes at home – simply open a can of curry sauce, add a few interesting ingredients and you have a wonderful meal.

NUTRITIONAL INFORMATION

Calories 513	Sugars 6g	
Protein 40g	Fat 27g	
Carbohydrate . . .30g	Saturates 8g	

15 mins   1 1/2 hours

SERVES 4

I N G R E D I E N T S

750 g/1 lb 10 oz lean lamb (from the leg)

3 tbsp ghee or vegetable oil

500 g/1 lb 2 oz potatoes, peeled and cut into large 2.5-cm/1-inch pieces

1 large onion, cut into quarters and sliced

2 garlic cloves, crushed

175 g/6 oz mushrooms, thickly sliced

280 g/10 oz canned Tikka Masala Curry Sauce

300 ml/10 fl oz water

3 tomatoes, halved and cut into thin slices

125 g/4½ oz spinach, washed and stalks trimmed

salt

sprigs of fresh mint, to garnish

1 Cut the lamb into 2.5-cm/1-inch cubes. Heat the ghee or oil in a large pan, add the lamb and cook over a moderate heat for 3 minutes or until sealed all over. Remove the lamb from the pan.

2 Add the potatoes, onion, garlic and mushrooms and cook for 3–4 minutes, stirring frequently.

3 Stir the curry sauce and water into the pan, add the lamb, mix well and season with salt to taste. Cover and cook very gently, stirring occasionally, for 1 hour or until the lamb is tender and cooked through.

4 Add the sliced tomatoes and the spinach to the pan, pushing the leaves well down into the mixture, then cover and cook for another 10 minutes until the spinach is cooked and tender.

5 Remove from the heat and transfer to serving plates. Garnish with sprigs of fresh mint and serve hot.

COOK'S TIP

Spinach leaves wilt quickly during cooking, so if the leaves are young and tender add them whole to the mixture; larger leaves may be coarsely shredded, if wished, before adding to the pan.

Potato Muffins

Using potatoes in sweet dishes may seem an odd idea, but, in fact, they add a lightness and lift to all kinds of baked goods.

NUTRITIONAL INFORMATION	
Calories 98	Sugars 11g
Protein 3g	Fat 2g
Carbohydrate ...18g	Saturates 0.5g

15 mins 30 mins

MAKES 12

I N G R E D I E N T S

butter, for greasing

75 g/2¾ oz self-raising flour, plus extra for dusting

175 g/6 oz floury potatoes, peeled

2 tbsp brown sugar

1 tsp baking powder

125 g/4½ oz raisins

4 eggs, separated

1 Lightly grease and flour a 12-cup muffin tin. Dice the potatoes and cook in a saucepan of boiling water for about 10 minutes or until tender. Drain thoroughly and mash until smooth.

2 Transfer the mashed potatoes to a mixing bowl and add the flour, sugar, baking powder, raisins and egg yolks. Stir well to mix thoroughly.

3 In a clean bowl, whisk the egg whites until they are standing in peaks. Using a metal spoon, gently fold them into the potato mixture until fully incorporated.

4 Divide the mixture among the 12 prepared cups in the muffin tin.

5 Cook in a preheated oven, 200°C/ 400°F/Gas Mark 6, for 10 minutes. Lower the oven temperature to 160°C/ 325°F/Gas Mark 3 and cook the muffins for 7–10 minutes or until risen.

6 Remove the muffins from the tin and serve warm.

  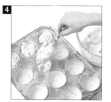

COOK'S TIP

Instead of spreading the muffins with plain butter, serve them with cinnamon butter made by blending 5 tablespoons of butter with a large pinch of ground cinnamon.